Witches!? In Salem?!
(A Brief & True Narrative Edition)

by Matt Cox

LICENSING & PRODUCTION INQUIRIES
Uproar Theatrics, LLC.
hello@uproartheatrics.com | www.UproarTheatrics.com

Witches!? In Salem?! copyright © 2024 by Matt Cox

Witches!? In Salem?! is published by Uproar Theatrics, LLC
500 8th Ave FRNT 3, #1714 New York, NY 10018

ISBN: 978-1-968051-16-7

First Printing, April 2025

WITCHES!? IN SALEM?! received its world premiere at HERE Arts Center in New York City on March 17th, 2024. The producers were Johnathan Cottle, Matt Cox, and Jake Keefe in association with Bonfire Works Foundation. It was directed by Rachel Dart; the stage manager was Vanessa Rebeil; the scenic, costume, and prop design was by K.C. McGeorge and Noah Ruff; the lighting design was by Johnathan Cottle; the sound design was by Matt Cox; original music was composed by Brian Metolius. Additional contributions to the script by Stephen Stout. The cast was as follows:

ANN PUTNAM JR. & OTHERS…Jessie Cannizzaro
SATAN…Matt Cox
THOMAS PUTNAM…Nick Carrillo
THE MAGISTRATE & OTHERS…AJ Ditty
MARY WARREN & OTHERS…Carolina Đỗ
COTTON MATHER & OTHERS… Aaron Parker Fouhey
REVEREND PARRIS…James Fouhey
EPHRAIM WILDES & OTHERS…Jake Keefe
JENNY ANNE & OTHERS…Andy Miller
ABIGAIL WILLIAMS & OTHERS…Jessica Mosher
BETTY PARRIS & OTHERS…Jordan Sison

The production was made possible by contributions on Indiegogo from:

MaryAnn Spencer	Zachary Kline
indiegogo	Jill Wolf
Dennis Corsi	nmredfield
Keith Rubin	Cecilia Tan
John Koblin	acody381
Janani Sreenivasan	Meghan Linehan
Anna Dart	Harrison Bryan
Gina Sarno	Liz Re
Anna Miles	Emily Schoen
Laurie Beckoff	Megan McDowell
Kelly Ellenwood	steoremus
Colin Waitt	Christopher DiMeglio
Michael Fynan	Robyne Martinez
Cheryl Webster Miller	Thomas Brudnicki
Francesca Pazniokas	Debbie Cox
Alex Tobey	Tzivia Kleinbart
Adam Salberg	Matt Castings
Giverny Petitmermet	Mark Weissglass
Melanie Queponds	Noel Cyr
Steph Jacobson	Kathryn Leep-Lazar
Alyssa Friday	Michael Weisner
Carrie Kei Heim	Brandon Cox
Teresa Langford	Molly Marinik
Autumn Heydt	Pamela Cottle
Heart of Gold	stephen rotan
Amanda Mouzakes	Preston Whiteway
irdart	Jessica Faust
Rachael Kinser	Michael Levinton
Eddie Ackley	Anthony Mercurio
Kylie Sinclair	cghansel
Ericka Morales	brian bauman
Kelly Ellenwood	John Brunner
Hampton Palmore	Eleanor Philips
Javier Antonio Gonzalez	Kyle Wade
Doyle Valley	Jacob Harvey
Kelly Ellenwood	orr y
David V Lu	Adam La Faci
Anthony Carro Jr	Greg Godbout
ucbgirlie	Jacob Baron
Brian Murphy	Philip Markle
Robby Carrillo	David Pasteelnick

Mike Axelrod
Jonathon Rosenthal
Austin Ruffer
Amy Ackerman
John Coons
pony (danny)
Debbie Cox
Henry Muller
Kelly Wolff
Ashlee Cantrell
Rachel Spina Kester
Adam Salberg
Elizabeth Tarsky
Robert Ribar
Julie Earls
Lauren Elder
Bonnie DiLorenzo
bgterrill
Peter Tatara
Nathaniel Foster
Sean Hoes
Benedict Rattray

Kaitlyn Walsh
jeffreyomura
Ben Rimalower
josephaaronpapa
Hank Balbirer
laurelstanley
Skylar Fox
Tina Fallon
MacKenzie Skye
Austin Kunis
kab69417
chiara.atik
Daniel Dobrovich
jordandene
Sarah Aitch-p
alison
Jared Griffin
Brandi-Leigh Miller
David Carpenter
Libby Rotan
Finn, Charlotte, Keith & Krista
Lisa Kerns

THANK YOU FOR YOUR CONTRIBUTIONS
MAKING THIS SHOW POSSIBLE!

<u>CHARACTERS/POTENTIAL TRACKS</u>

Doubling below reflective of the original production. Feel free to cast more actors and mix / match roles to suit your needs.

TRACK 1:
THOMAS PUTNAM: A conniving, greedy soul who will do what it takes to get what he wants. His plot goes awry immediately, but he does his best to keep up with it throughout the play.

TRACK 2:
REVEREND PARRIS: A spineless, petty narcissist of a Reverend who cares most about his personal needs, gains, and firewood. He demands a respect no one gives him, at least until he becomes the defacto spiritual leader braving the new discovered evil within the village.

TRACK 3:
BELLA'LOCH: Your stereotypical witch living her life. Has some concerns about being discovered, but isn't too worried.

TRACK 4:
XANATAR: Your stereotypical wizard. Is loving this Salem place.
JOHN PROCTOR: A real everyman, leading actor type. Loves a good powerful monologue.
UNNAMED VILLAGER: A villager with some accusations to throw around.

TRACK 5:

ABIGAIL WILLIAMS: A twelve year old girl who has seen some stuff. Intelligent, perhaps too intelligent for her own good.

GOODY GOOD: A messy street vagrant. Loves the sound of her own name.

SARAH DUSTIN: A rather ordinary woman who finds herself on the wrong side of the law.

TRACK 6:

BETTY PARRIS: The Reverend's daughter. Full of confidence and nerves and the proper fear of God.

BRIDGET BISHOP: A village woman who has been through this before. Tired, confused, hoping for the best.

LYDIA DUSTIN: Quick to point fingers. Is always sending thoughts and prayers, and wants everyone to know it.

TRACK 7:

MARY WARREN: An awkward teenager of the village. She struggles with public speaking and also public accusings of her neighbors of being witches.

FARMER JOHN #1: A simple farmer with not many opinions.

MARTHA COREY: A gospel woman.

TRACK 8:

ANN PUTNAM JR.: A frightening child - very intense. A bit like she crawled out of a horror movie.

REBECCA NURSE: The kindest, oldest woman in Salem. Great at bringing a room full of people together.

FARMER GEORGE: A simple farmer with one concern: farming rye.

TRACK 9:
THE MAGISTRATE: An amalgamation of various magistrates, judges, and more. A monster delivering their own form of justice.
DOCTOR GRIGGS: An old doctor who really loves getting paid.
EDWARD BISHOP: A member of the Salem congregation with lots of loud and aggressive opinions.
FARMER JOHN #2: A simple farmer without too many opinions.

TRACK 10:
EPHRAIM WILDES: A constable lacking confidence and conviction. Really wants to get paid above all else, but doesn't love people being angry at him.
GOVERNOR PHIPS: A dandy English gentleman. Not a lot of government experience.

… And then BOSTONIANS & VILLAGERS to your heart's content / your own needs.

NOTES

First off, hello! Welcome to the 'Brief & True' edition of Witches!? In Salem?! This is an abridged 'one-act' version of the script - I've made several changes to the base play to attempt to deliver this concise version. The focus here is on depicting the actual events of the trials, with a few not-accurate characters thrown in for good measure. For full context, I would recommend looking at the full play just to understand the original intent of the scenes. That said, I do believe this version manages to give most characters a full arc. If your intent is to perform this version in a timed competition - additional cuts may be necessary. Feel free to cut, no additional permissions from Uproar needed. Lines must still be performed sequentially as written, and words may not be changed or substituted without prior written approval.

Some things to keep in mind:

/: denotes two characters speak at the same time.

The words "Witches In Salem": The original intent was for there to be a dramatic stinger of varying lengths everytime this phrase is used (with any sort of punctuation.) It's not completely necessary if you don't want it, but it is sort of built into the rhythm of the lines. I'd advise doing some version of that.

A note on hangings: feel free to depict these however you'd like to your comfort level. It can be as little as a light shift or a sound cue.

SCENE: THE PARRIS HOUSEHOLD - 1692

*BETTY PARRIS, lies FROZEN in bed. An
uncomfortable and unnatural position.
REVEREND PARRIS stands by her. ABIGAIL
sits in a corner. DR. GRIGGS, too old and not
fully 'here,' examines BETTY for a moment -
using OLD & STRANGE tools.*

Eventually...
DOCTOR GRIGGS
Welp. It's Witches. Witches. In Salem!
(a dramatic beat)
Yep. A hand is upon her, Mister Parris. The EVIL HAND.
And that's a diagnosis and one diagnosis means one payment
so -

REVEREND PARRIS
No. No, Dr. Griggs! Check her again! I'm sure it's some sort
of less severe affliction. Like a plague or…

DOCTOR GRIGGS
REVEREND. I'm a DOCTOR. That you'd imply I'd falsify
some sort of SPECTRAL AFFLICTION invisible to the
naked eye so I might PROFIT from it because I'm tired and
confused and I love coin so much I'd LIE to get more of it -
Wow. Afore you ask me for any further clarifications I'd be
asking how your Betty found herself under the EVIL HAND
in the first place - who she was with, what she was doing
mmhhmm but not until we finalize pay-

REVEREND PARRIS
ABIGAIL.

ABIGAIL WILLIAMS
Uncle, what ever could you w-

REVEREND PARRIS
YOU TELL ME WHAT YOU KNOW ABOUT BETTY SO I
MIGHT PUNISH YOU.

ABIGAIL WILLIAMS
Fine, I'll tell you everything.

REVEREND PARRIS
SILENCE! I DON'T WANT YOUR EXCUSES, you
horrible girl!

ABIGAIL WILLIAMS
No, there's a reasonable explanation for -

REVEREND PARRIS
SHHHHHHHH. Why aren't you giving me an answer?!

ABIGAIL WILLIAMS
I'm try - We only/ We - Look - no - listen to - we didn't -

REVEREND PARRIS
/OUT WITH IT, SPEAK! WHY ARE YOU SPEAKING?! I
DEMAND SILENCE!

ABIGAIL WILLIAMS
SHUT UP FOR ONCE AND LET ANYONE ELSE TALK.
WE ALL HEAR YOU BLATHER ON ENOUGH YOU
USELESS *CUMBERGROUNDLY FOPDOODLE!*

PARRIS and GRIGGS gasp.

REVEREND PARRIS
*The 'f' word preceded by the 'C' word? In my house? Oh
you're punishment shall be so, JOB himself will believe he
got off easy.*

2

ABIGAIL WILLIAMS

No, no. You misheard sir, see, I didn't mean to say that out loud - what I meant by it was uhm - uhm -

(Desperate, ABIGAIL makes a strong choice)

Ah! Please! Don't make *ME* SAY anything else - SATAN. Uh oh more is coming out: NO ONE LIKES LISTENING TO YOU UNCLE, you TAWDRY VILLAIN! Oh gosh! Pinches all over my body? It's so cold. NO, it's HOT? Ohh no my neck - It's twisting all the way around! WOOF. WOOF. Oh, so weak.

ABIGAIL falls on the bed. DR. GRIGGS 'examines her.'

DOCTOR GRIGGS

Welp. Looks like a case of more witches. In SALEM!...My work here is done. Now, remind me how I got in here and where I live?

PARRIS moves towards GRIGGS, coddling him.

REVEREND PARRIS

Wait wait wait, William. You're one of my favorite villagers, you know. Ye wouldn't utter a word of this to a soul, right? This tiny little 'situation.' We don't word of this to spread, no. Noooo. You know people like to talk. About me. I mean who wouldn't. Please. Not one word?

DOCTOR GRIGGS

Reverend. *Not. One. Word.*

They stare each other down. GRIGGS slowly backs his way offstage, maintaining eye contact. As he is close to exit, he turns and bolts off.

3

DOCTOR GRIGGS (O.S.)
WITCHE-

THOMAS PUTNAM enters in a flurry.

THOMAS PUTNAM
What's this I'm hearing about witches, Sam?

REVEREND PARRIS
Thomas Putnam! Sir. You. How?

THOMAS PUTNAM
I heard from my brother who heard from our uncle who
heard from my cousin who heard Giles Corey shouting on
horseback who heard from Doctor Griggs.
(towards the girls:)
O! THE PRECIOUS GIFT OF LIFE drained from the
INNOCENT. *Can they hear us?*

REVEREND PARRIS
If they could they'd have told us by now so we might punish
them for this horrible display of idleness.

THOMAS PUTNAM
Right. Sam! AHHH! This is to be our DOOM. I brought you
to SALEM. What do you give me in return? Sick witch kids!
This is the exact happenstance the PORTER FAMILY has
been waiting for to bring me down. You know the
PORTERS. We all know the PORTERS. The mortal enemy
of the GLORIOUS PUTNAM FAMILY. The cause of all
things evil in SALEM. Swindlers! Villains. *Porters.*

BOTH wallow not quite to each other.

REVEREND PARRIS
O, why must these PORTERS ruin everything?

THOMAS PUTNAM
O! Everything evil hides roots tied to that wretched family. *The Porters.*

REVEREND PARRIS
O, I thought this reverend thing was my life's calling -

THOMAS PUTNAM
O, you know what the Porters did.

REVEREND PARRIS
O, but here in Salem these horrid villagers conspire against me - they won't even pay me my firewood, the firewood we agreed upon via my contract -

THOMAS PUTNAM
O! We all know what the PORTERS did...

REVEREND PARRIS
"Ohhh, Reverend Parris only cares about his SALARY," They say! I care about plenty of things. But also, where's my SALARY?

THOMAS PUTNAM
O woe woe! The hardships I endure daily! BEING SECOND RICHEST MAN Slash Second Largest Landowner in SALEM? BEHIND WHOM? I'LL GIVE YOU TWO GUESS- THE PORTERS!
                    (together:)
/O, Why must life be so hard for men in 1692?

REVEREND PARRIS
/O, Why must life be so hard for men in 1692?

THOMAS PUTNAM
…It is witches for certain?

REVEREND PARRIS
Griggs diagnosed it so. He said he'd never falsify some sort of SPECTRAL AFFLICTION invisible to the naked eye so he might PROFIT from it. I mean, who would ever do that?

THOMAS PUTNAM
Wait! That could work. Wait, no way. Unless? Yep. First thought best thought - Sam ...There may be a way we can both get what we want out of this. ...and so much more.

REVEREND PARRIS
My salary? My contractually obligated firewood? Tell me if you mean my firewood.

THOMAS PUTNAM
Sure, Sam. Your firewood. Your precious firewood. Come! We must act in haste. *I* need to get out of here before I am seen. And *you* need to tell the villagers *the truth. Now.*

REVEREND PARRIS
I'm sorry - The *truth?*

THOMAS PUTNAM
Mmmhhhmm. Hahaha! HAHAHA!

> *PUTNAM exits. PARRIS, a bit confused, turns to Betty.*

REVEREND PARRIS
Betty? Please, Betty. Sit up? *You have chores to do.*

> *PARRIS sighs and exits.*

> *A long beat. BETTY sits up with a GASP. ABIGAIL too. They look at one another. They scream.*

SCENE: SALEM VILLAGE CHURCH / MEETINGHOUSE

> *VILLAGERS enter, joining the screaming / doing whatever scenic changes may be necessary. Eventually, all turn to say:*

ALL VILLAGERS OF SALEM
WITCHES!?

> *CHAOS and NOISE as MANY take places all around the theater. The entire room becomes the SALEM VILLAGE CHURCH/ MEETINGHOUSE.*

> *PARRIS stands at a pulpit, yelling at everyone.*

REVEREND PARRIS
NOTHING IS CONFIRMED! IT'S NOT NOT CONFIRMED EITHER BUT: CALM! *CALM* **CALM!**

> *All calmed down at some point in the middle of this spectacle.*

REVEREND PARRIS
Thank ye for calming down. I will now finish the sentence I had begun before such a raucous reaction did occur, preventing me from finishing the remark.
> (clears his throat)

In Salem.

MARTHA COREY
Except it doesn't sound like we have witches in Salem. More like it's witches In Parris' house.

MANY MEMBERS OF THE CONGREGATION
(some semblance of:)
YEAH, HE'S THE WORST! / BOO PARRIS! / *GOODY COREY JUST GOT YOU.*

REVEREND PARRIS
T'is no time for anyone to point fingers. Because frankly, this is on ALL OF YOU!
(so much pointing)
Your SQUABBLES, your SINS, your refusal to give contractually owed firewood - that's what brought SATAN ALLEGEDLY here!

MANY MEMBERS OF THE CONGREGATION
BOOOOOOO!

REVEREND PARRIS
I'll give something to BOO about!

PARRIS charges into the congregation. FIGHTS break out.

ALL VILLAGERS OF SALEM
FIGHT! / THIS IS A LAWSUIT! / BOOOOOO! [etc.]

REBECCA NURSE stands. Kind.

REBECCA NURSE
Please... Everyone...

EDWARD BISHOP
Shh - Rebecca Nurse has something to say.

REBECCA NURSE
Each of us is alive. Our time in this prison called life is fleeting. It is precious. So why fill these living breaths with

REBECCA NURSE (CONT)

something so vile as hate? We weren't made to handle hate. We were built to love. To ease each other's burdens. Aye, now that takes more effort in a world that asks so much of us already. Yet still, I shall love my GOD. I shall LOVE my neighbors. I shall choose: LOVE. Will you choose it too?

ALL VILLAGERS

[Chuckle] / Oh, Rebecca Nurse. / *She's right.* / I'm sorry I choked you. [etc.]

THOMAS PUTNAM

Please. Everyone. Before you calm down, know that what Reverend Parris is saying is: he loves you. He was just telling me earlier how love is love is love. But I won't hear him be told by anyone, *Rebecca*, that his HATE be wrong - for he hates SATAN and any who would scheme with the enemy. FOR RANDOM EXAMPLE if you told me, I don't know, THE PORTERS are involved, which I'm not saying that the PORTERS are aligned with the devil. However, the first thing I'd do when we found out *the Porters were aligned with the devil* would not be to love them. No! I'd pray their evilly earned bank accounts be divided amongst us who suffer by their hand & their LANDS forfeited to those who live righteously! Someone like, I don't know, me. These aren't my words. Nay. They are Reverend Parris'.

REVEREND PARRIS

They are.

THOMAS PUTNAM

Parris bravely stands before us today in defiance of The Devil! His poor children lie at the center of this hellish plot. Before ye complain of Mister Parris, Consider his children.

EDWARD BISHOP
I GOT SOMETHING TO SAY.

THOMAS PUTNAM
Did you consider his poor children being tortured by Satan?

EDWARD BISHOP
I HAVE NOTHING TO SAY.

THOMAS PUTNAM
But WHO could have sicked Satan on them, huh? We've already got the PORTER theory, I don't remember who brought that up, that's worth thinking about. WHO else, Mister Parris?

REVEREND PARRIS
(flips through the BIBLE)
...Only a "child of THE DEVIL and enemy of all things GOOD!"

> GOODY GOOD enters. A bit dirty. A bit
> unkempt.

GOODY GOOD
Yessss? Someone shoutin' for me in here?

REVEREND PARRIS
[sigh.] No one called for you, Sarah Good.

GOODY GOOD
Yesss - There it is again - I heard my name. Someone said it.

REVEREND PARRIS
I did. But the first time was not in reference to you, it's a frequent word we use.

GOODY GOOD

What word?

REVEREND PARRIS

Good.

GOODY GOOD

Yeees?

THOMAS PUTNAM

Don't you have things to be doing out in the filthy streets?
Maybe, I don't know, ruining the whole village, Goody
Good?

GOODY GOOD

Yesss. Oh - Rude. DON'T NONE A' YOU GO BOTHERIN'
ASKING ME TO STAY. Cause. If you dids, you know what
I'd say? "I'm *good.*"
　　　　　(exits muttering)
Yesss? Ooo, look, I did it to myself. Huh, makes ya think.

She exits mumbling under her breath.

THOMAS PUTNAM

Okay, I'm not saying *Sarah Good/ is a witch.* But - Sarah
Good/... Witch?

GOODY GOOD pops on for each 'Good.'

GOODY GOOD

/Yes? /Yessss?

THOMAS PUTNAM

O LORD! It is becoming clear to me that there is an enemy
present here in Salem. The Enemy. Tell us Mister Parris,
what can we do?!

REVEREND PARRIS
I. Don't. Know.

THOMAS PUTNAM
THESE ARE YOUR WORDS, REVEREND! TELL US
WHAT TO DO!

REVEREND PARRIS
(opens the bible, searches)
Uhm. "be swift to hear, slow to speak, and slow to wrath-"

THOMAS PUTNAM
No. Further back - Back towards the beginning!

REVEREND PARRIS
Ah! "Thou shalt not suffer *a witch* to live."

THOMAS PUTNAM
AND SO WE SHAN'T SUFFER A SINGLE WITCH IN
SALE-

*From the back of the room, BELLA'LOCH
enters. She is very clearly a witch. The most
stereotypical of witches.*

BELLA'LOCH
AHAHAHA! Oh no! I'm so SORRY my dearies. You've
begun! How rude of me. "Good morrow, fellow villagers!"
Wow - *Love the bonnets I'm seeing today. Goody. Goody.
Hello to all Goodies, and non Goodies.* What have I missed
here in my favorite place - *churk? Am I pronouncing that
correctly? Churk.*

THOMAS PUTNAM
Goody Bloodkraven. Mr. Parris, in his own words, hath
revealed we be a'plagued. By WITCHES! In Salem.

ALL VILLAGERS OF SALEM
(With so much vitriol)
WITCHES! IN SALEM!

*All look to BELLA. Bella takes a moment to
process.*

BELLA'LOCH
...WhAaaaAaaAt?!? Nooooooo! *Noo!* Witches, huh? *Witches
witches!?* In Salem Salem?! Wow. Wow wow wow. WOW
everyone's heard about these Witches? And, this is a bad
thing? YES, I see by your expressions, THIS. IS. A BAD.
THING. Oof! Grrr! Yikes! I, I! I. *I am speechless.*
(a beat)
Seems like Churck is done, unrelated reasons I have to r-

XANATAR enters, very clearly a wizard.

XANATAR
AH HA! GOOD MORROW MY DEAREST VILLAGERS
OF SALEM. Sorry to be TARDY. Though the winds of time
are a fickle thing I say.

BELLA'LOCH
"Husband" Xanatar, actually no you uh -

XANATAR
I hope I haven't delayed any chanting of the puh-salms.
Everyone seems upset. As usual.

BELLA'LOCH
Xanatar - you won't believe this - Mr. Putname has declared
there be *Witches.*

ALL VILLAGERS
IN SALEM!

XANATAR
...WhAAaat?? Nooooooo. *Noo!* No. I DON'T SEE ANY! I
NEVER HAVE! Wow. Wow, wow, wow, wow, wow wow
wow. I. *I.* I am so upset. ...We gotta KILL these witches.

BELLA'LOCH
Yes, Xanatar, I CANNOT SIT IDLY WHILST WITCHES
are outside. We need to - HUNT THEM.

XANATAR
YEAH a regular ol' - I don't know if there's a phrase for it -

XANATAR & BELLA
A witch looky look look. That's what WE NEED!
WITCHES?! WITCHES!!!!

> *They're gone. A long suspenseful beat. All look
> off after them.*

THOMAS PUTNAM
Did ...you all witness what I just did? Our newest neighbors,
Goody Bella'Loch'Du'Lochich Bloodkraven and Goodman
Xanatar 'The Blue' BloodKraven, they...
              (to the congregation)
They put you all to shame. That is the ZEAL such so called
people of FAITH should be showing when presented with
the FACTS you have. How shameful for you.

EDWARD BISHOP
Let's hit witches with sticks! I got a stick right here! I'll start
hitting!

LYDIA DUSTIN
I am actively sending thoughts and prayers to all victims.

MARTHA COREY
Please! We ought to be asking questions before we rush to blame - any questions! The last thing we need is a crazed village full of rumor.

THOMAS PUTNAM
(to an audience member or an extra congregation member)
That guy told me the witches eat babies.

THE VILLAGE
[Gasp!] Not our babies!

EDWARD BISHOP
We need someone to guide us through this devilish time. We NEED TO LISTEN TO REVEREND PARRIS.

REVEREND PARRIS
I - wha?

LYDIA DUSTIN
To think of his poor children shivering in the terrible cold. To think of him enduring that same cold...

EDWARD BISHOP
The least we can do is pay our share of firewood.

REVEREND PARRIS
My salary? My wood?
(a beat)
IT'S WITCHES, ALRIGHT. The devil, he's HERE. And he wants to do bad stuff. End of SERM-

LYDIA DUSTIN
But wait - Mr. Putnam! How is your daughter? Is ANN JR well?

THOMAS PUTNAM

Oh she's fi-noooo! She's been in bed all day. Strange fever. Dog barks. Head fully twisting all the way around all creepy. It couldn't be. Or could it?

REVEREND PARRIS

Thomas you didn't mention -

THOMAS PUTNAM

I must away. To check on my Ann! End of sermon.

EDWARD BISHOP

I'm going to get more sticks! We're all gonna need them!

LYDIA DUSTIN

That Martha Corey sure was asking a lot of questions, huh?

MARTHA COREY

But - Oh, I have a bad feeling about this Rebecca.

REBECCA NURSE

I'm sorry. My ears don't work so well. Is everyone loving each other now?

ALL but PARRIS have made their way OFF.

REVEREND PARRIS

Uh, Amen - Thank you all for -
                    (to himself + to the heavens)
It all adds up when you think about it. T'is but a test of my own saintliness! Of course!
                    (sinister)
And I'll have the respect I'm due. I'll have *MY salary. And oh - I'll have my WOOD. Mmm. Yes. Very...*
                    (he looks around)
Good.

GOODY GOOD appears behind him.

GOODY GOOD

Yeeeesss?

Parris shrieks.

SCENE: LATER - A SCENE OF FARMERS

FARMERS do farm work. Perhaps they all rake at nothing. Perhaps they do other work farmers would do.

FARMER JOHN #1

Say, John -

FARMER JOHN #2

/Yeah?

JOHN PROCTOR

/Yes?

FARMER JOHN #1
(to FARMER #1)
Sorry. This John. Whatcha think about these witches?

FARMER JOHN #2
Mmm. Don't much know, John. Don't much care.

FARMER JOHN #1

Yeah. Say, John -

FARMER JOHN #2

Yeah?

JOHN PROCTOR
Yes?

FARMER JOHN #1
Sorry, John Proctor. What you think about these witches?

JOHN PROCTOR
Putnam and Parris stirring up troubles, nothing more. I could
go on about it - which I will: A MAN MAY THINK GOD
SLEEPS BUT -

FARMER JOHN #1
No need to monologue today, Proctor. How about you,
George? What do you think about the witches?

FARMER GEORGE
I have nothing to say about nothing lest it's in regards to me
and farming my Rye. The primary crop of Salem.

ALL
Mhm. True facts.

> *BRIDGET BISHOP enters. A normal, but
> stressed, woman. She carries something, also
> doing work.*

BRIDGET BISHOP
Good morrow, Gentleman.

3 JOHNS & A GEORGE
Good morrow, Bridget Bishop.

BRIDGET BISHOP
Say, Johns.

ALL JOHNS

Yes?

BRIDGET BISHOP

You heard about the witches?

JOHN PROCTOR

Don't pay a care to any word PUTNAM says.

BRIDGET BISHOP

Right. Of course.
                    (a beat)
....Everyone knows I'm not a witch, right? We went through
the whole ordeal ten years ago. What when I was accused of
'being a witch.' Remember? There was a trial. A lot of mean
things were said. At me. Because I 'wore red.' We all
remember that, right?

CONSTABLE EPHRAIM WILDES enters.

EPHRAIM WILDES

Morrow gentleman! Goody Bishop. Working hard or are you
hard working?

PROCTOR & ALL FARMERS & BRIDGET

Constable / Ephraim / Mr. Wildes.

EPHRAIM WILDES

You all heard about the witches?

ALL ON STAGE

Mhhhm.

BRIDGET BISHOP

Not like history repeats itself or anything ever. Right?

EPHRAIM WILDES

They don't got any evidence of these Sarah's BEING witches. So. Can't do any arresting - nuh huh. Which is a real shame. After all, I really only get paid when I have prisoners in jail.

FARMER JOHN #2

What The Town pays you per prisoner?

EPHRAIM WILDES

No - no, The Prisoners. THEY pay me to be imprisoned by me. They pay for their own food, their blankets, having a bed. I'm told it makes a whole lot of sense.

FARMER GEORGE

Well, the rye over yonder won't tend to itself, no no.

JOHNS, BRIDGET, AND WILDES
GEORGE.

GEORGE exits.

BRIDGET BISHOP

You know what's not fun? Being arrested for being a witch. Which we all remember: I am not.

JOHNS & EPHRAIM

Mhhhm.

EPHRAIM WILDES

If you ask me this whole thing will blow over. I've got a good sense for this kind of stuff.

THUNDER.

EPHRAIM WILDES
Uh oh. Guess it's going to rain. That's sudden. Strange.

SCENE: PUTNAMS

*A BIRD flutters on. A harmless ten year old
enters, carrying a bag. ANN PUTNAM JR. She
moves towards the bird. Holds out her hands.
The bird flies to her. She handles it delicately.
Then cracks its neck. She giggles whilst expertly
tearing its wings. She kneels to the ground and
dumps the contents of her bag out. SO MANY
DEAD BIRDS. THOMAS enters.*

THOMAS PUTNAM
Okay, Thomas. She's only your daughter, you can talk to -

ANN PUTNAM JR
Hello, Thomas Putnam.

THOMAS PUTNAM
Ahhh! I mean - ahhh. My dear ANN Jr.

ANN PUTNAM JR
Earthly father, gaze upon how my collection grows.

THOMAS PUTNAM
Wow. So... coool. Eh hem. OH ANN.

He begins to 'weep' - overacting quite a bit.

ANN PUTNAM JR
Mister Thomas Putnam - you weep?

THOMAS PUTNAM

You weren't supposed to see my tears, ANN JR. But O, I DO
WEEP! I weep for you, child! But twelve and your life is
over because of all the terrible things THE PORTER'S have
done. I weep for we live in squalor! Second richest family in
Salem? We're this close to living on the streets like... *Sarah
Good.*

GOODY GOOD
(appearing, whispered)

Yesss?

ANN PUTNAM JR

If only the despots and Irish and Porters of the world would
be punished righteously by the hand that is holy.

THOMAS PUTNAM

Funny you mention that, Ann Jr. The other day weren't you
telling me you were beset upon my evil spirits in your sleep?

ANN PUTNAM JR

No?

THOMAS PUTNAM

What?! YES. Yes you were! You went on and on about how
various landowners and businessmen and their wives and
some general vagrant types tortured you! How could you
forget it, child?!

ANN PUTNAM JR

I don't - Could Satan have made me forget?

THOMAS PUTNAM

He must have! Please ANN JR. Let me help you remember
everything that happened. In vivid and graphic detail. For the
village. For we, the Putnams... Ha. Haha. HAHAHAHA!

SCENE: ANOTHER PERSPECTIVE

MARY enters.

MARY WARREN

Hello. I'm Mary Warren. I'm eighteen. I live in Salem
Village. I work at the Proctor's house. I have no other things
to say. Wow, thank you for listening. No one has really
listened that much before. Feels good. *But not in a sinful way
- no!*
>   (a beat)
By chance have you heard about the witches? Wow, huh?
Crazy. Like everyone is saying: What is happening to our
village? This place used to be perfect. Maybe not perfect for
"everyone." Me for instance. Not to go on about myself but
there's nobody my age in the village who aren't spoken for
or dead from all the wars. Don't worry, I'm fine - I've been
resigned to dying alone since I was seven or so. Yet -
because I have this awful need for human interaction I hang
out with Abigail Williams and Betty Parris. Who are twelve
and nine. Which is fine, eighteen year olds and nine and
twelve year olds have much in common. I avoid Ann Putnam
Jr. I find her... unnatural. ...Options are a scarcity here in our
lives. See, a typical boys day in Salem: they get to go hunt,
or fish, or HIT STUFF REALLY HARD WITH HAMMERS
ALL DAY. We are meant to sit. Sew stuff. Fold things. And
hit nothing with hammers.
>   (a beat then spilling out)
I've been hiding something from you, which is terrible
because you've been kind. Do you ever wonder about good
and evil and consequences for your actions? Me too, all the
time. Which brings me to this CONFESSION. I've done
something terrible. Forsooth, I was there when all this began.
BEHOLD. Bare witness to that which occurred a day before
anyone cried 'witches!' Me and Abigail and Betty were at
Reverend Parris' house when -

SCENE: PARRIS' HOUSE - A FLASHBACK

MARY turns, ABIGAIL & BETTY enter. A scene from a few weeks prior. They look around to ensure they are alone. The scene has an air of secrecy throughout.

ABIGAIL WILLIAMS
Psst. Mary. *Lubberwort says what.*

MARY WARREN
Uh ...Wha?

ABIGAIL WILLIAMS
Ha - Mary's a lubberwort. She said it herself - she said whaaa?

BETTY PARRIS
Nice one Abby! Mary, you fudging Lubberwort. Heck!

ABIGAIL & BETTY laugh, but quietly.

ABIGAIL WILLIAMS
Mary. We're gonna put egg whites into a glass of water so we can find out what our future husband's occupations will be.

BETTY PARRIS
It's called a Venus Glass. I bet you didn't even know that. It's gonna be cah-razy

ABIGAIL WILLIAMS
You in, ya old maid?

MARY WARREN
Isn't that fortune telling? Is that allowed?

ABIGAIL WILLIAMS
O.M. Lord and savior, Don't be so MARY about this. Throw prudence to the winds! Learn to live a little.

BETTY PARRIS
Learn to live you lubberwort.

MARY WARREN
(to us:)
Hey, have you ever met a really confident child? These two, they're really confident children.
(back to scene - she is handed a glass and and 'egg')
YEAH I'LL play I'm COOL I'm OLD, gal pals.

BETTY PARRIS
ME FIRST! I bet my future husband's gonna be like a hunkin' Potter. *Making bowls out of clay. He'll be like uh yeah watch me work my profession. Uh uh uh.*
(a beat)
We already know who ABIGAIL's husband will be.......

PROCTOR appears behind a WINDOW, or just out and about.

BETTY PARRIS
Look, it's Jooooohn Proctor.

MARY WARREN
Good morrow, Mister Proctor.

JOHN PROCTOR
What? What are you? Ohhh No.... No. No no no. Noooo.

PROCTOR exits.

ABIGAIL WILLIAMS
Ew. No. I don't even know that old man. *MARY. CRACK THE EGG ALREADY.*

They hold up a glass of water. MARY hesitates... Then cracks the egg.

ABIGAIL WILLIAMS
So - What do you see?

MARY WARREN
It almost looks like - a coffin?

BETTY PARRIS
...Well now I only see a coffin. What's it mean? What's a COFFIN MEAN?!

MARY WARREN
A sign of EVIL? Or DEATH? What devilry have I done?!

MARY & BETTY scream.

REVEREND PARRIS (OFF)
Why do I hear NOISE in MY HOUSE?

ABIGAIL WILLIAMS
Hey - calm it down. It's an egg. It can't hurt you.

BETTY PARRIS
OH geez oh geez oh geez. Evil is sin punished with HECKFIRE.
            (she slaps herself)
I'm THE REVEREND'S daughter. I'm to emulate

BETTY PARRIS (CONT)

GODLINESS. If he sees me in here with an EGG in a
GLASS - ohhhhh geez

(slaps herself again)

Then again if I wasn't one of the saints chosen to go to
Heaven when Heaven was created in the first place I'm
already going to HECK no matter how I behave my whole
whole life and maybe the coffin means SOON geez O Geez
O aaaaaah eeeeeeeeeeeee - So. Much. Press- ure.

BETTY twitches and FREEZES. A genuine fit.

ABIGAIL WILLIAMS

Betty?

*ABIGAIL and MARY look to one another. Then
to BETTY. Then to one another. MARY, back to
us:*

MARY WARREN

Yeaaah so as YOU may have heard - days later it's
WITCHCRAFT being cried. Now you're caught up. And
now YOU know the truth. It was all my fault. I cracked the
egg. I let evil into our village. I let it harm my... my best
friends. I must be punished. I must confess. Mister Parris! I
must speak to you without DELAY.

*PARRIS has entered, clutching a log of
FIREWOOD tight.*

REVEREND PARRIS

Woah. You're being a lot right now. I was searching for you,
Warren. Come with me! To right over there. SIT.

SCENE: THE MAGISTRATE COMETH

> *MARY looks to where BETTY sits FROZEN next to ABIGAIL covered in blankets. MARY squeezes between.*

REVEREND PARRIS
ABIGAIL tells me you too have fallen ill at the, uh, hands of the devil?

MARY WARREN
uhhhhhuhhh heeeey, *ABIGAIL? Can we talk outside for one sec -*

ABIGAIL WILLIAMS
shutupMary. Uncle - we're so cold. Might we light a fire?

REVEREND PARRIS
You don't burn spruce such as this. You cherish it.
(to the wood)
No no, don't listen to her. Shh - you're safe with me.

> *PARRIS exits. BETTY springs to life.*

BETTY PARRIS
Ow, it's getting really hard to hold this, Abby.

> *MARY screams at BETTY. BETTY screams at MARY. ABIGAIL covers both their mouths.*

MARY WARREN
Whaaaat is happening?!

ABIGAIL WILLIAMS
Mary you gotta be cool here, k? I've got it all planned out.

MARY WARREN

A plan? There's a plan?

ABIGAIL WILLIAMS

The Devil's 'Witches' made BETTY freak out and LAY IN BED for a whole day, who does that?

BETTY PARRIS

There was so much pressure - I'm NINE.

ABIGAIL WILLIAMS

NEXT: these 'Witches' made me say stuff about Uncle Parris that you can never ever say out loud. ONLY the thing is - when you're beset by witches - YOU CAN say it. Watch: UNCLE!!!

PARRIS rushes on.

ABIGAIL WILLIAMS

You CALF LOLLY! YOU DANDY PRAT!

REVEREND PARRIS

Curse ye, Satan!

He exits. BETTY unfreezes. ABIGAIL giggles.

ABIGAIL WILLIAMS

See? When SATAN makes you do something bad - no one gets mad at *you*. It's Satan's fault!

MARY WARREN

Okay. So do we have witches forever?

ABIGAIL WILLIAMS
I dunno - do you want to sleep past dawn forever? Spend your afternoons not sewing or folding or choring forever? Speak in more than a HUSHED WHISPER and have people actually LISTEN?!

MARY WARREN
So why do I have witches?

ABIGAIL WILLIAMS
Why wouldn't you WANT to?! Mary, You of all people need a break. Look, eventually, if it has to - the curse can be lifted or whatever so that everyone may rejoice for we no longer suffer. A miracle! There's literally no downside here. It's a victimless win for everyone.

BETTY PARRIS
Trust Abigail, Mary. She's twelve. She knows stuff.

MARY WARREN
But the Egg. I cracked the egg. THE EGG.

ABIGAIL WILLIAMS
Why are you talking about EGGS Mar-

PARRIS enters, ABIGAIL scrambles up. BETTY refreezes.

ABIGAIL WILLIAMS
GO YOUR OWN WAY YOU OAFISH MISERABLE GOLLUMPUS of an uncle.
(cough)
These witches.

REVEREND PARRIS
The 'G' word? Sir. I'm sorry you had to hear that.

THE MAGISTRATE enters. The most PURITAN of PURITANS.

THE MAGISTRATE

Hrrrm.

REVEREND PARRIS

Girls. A Magistrate has arrived to our Village. He's come to, what was it again, sir?

THE MAGISTRATE

Interrogate the afflicted children. Most. Thoroughly.

MARY WARREN

ABIGAIL, how about that talk out-

ABIGAIL WILLIAMS

shutupMary.

REVEREND PARRIS

You do as Magistrate Hathorne asks. Or are you Magistrate Corwin?

THE MAGISTRATE

The answer is both. We are both men. For we are a theatrical construct - an amalgamation of souls, a merging of consciences, parading around in a false human carcass. CALL US THE MAGISTRATE. SALEM'S MOST OFFICIAL OFFICIAL OF THE LAW.
(turns to the GIRLS)
Hello Children. Call me your Friendly Village The Magistrate. And then tell me: WHO DID THIS TO YOU?! WHO BEWITCHED YOU?! WHY AREN'T YOU ANSWERING?! ARE YOU SHAMMING!? ARE YOU FILTHY SHAMMING CHILDREN?! DO WE HAVE TO TORTURE YOU OR LOCK YOU UP TIL YOU SPEAK

THE MAGISTRATE (CONT)
NOT SHAM IN ANSWER?!

BETTY PARRIS
OH MY GOD -

REVEREND PARRIS
BETTY! She speaks! A miracle! Can she do some chores for
me?

THE MAGISTRATE
No! BETTY! CONFESS. WHO BEWITCHED YOU?!
WHO WHO WHO?!

BETTY PARRIS
Ahhhhhhhh -

THE MAGISTRATE
MARY WARREN - YOU AREN'T TALKING! DO YOU
WANT ME TO LOCK **YOU** IN A PRISON CELL WHERE
YOU'LL DIE? - SAY A NAME, JUST TO PROVE YOU
KNOW WHAT A NAME IS.

MARY WARREN
SARAH-isacommonname?!

THE MAGISTRATE
WHICH SARAH DO YE NAME? Any of ye NAME ME A
SARAH. ANY SARAH.

The girls sit stunned.

THE MAGISTRATE
BE THIS SOME SHAM? - THE PENALTY FOR MAKING
SHAM IS DEATH!

MARY WARREN
Abigail? Can we please speak outs-

ABIGAIL WILLIAMS
ShutupMary. How about we all calm down here and - Oh
Fine! Uncle Parris. Maybe we should speak -

ANN PUTNAM JR. enters.

ANN PUTNAM JR
Truth be told, I've seen many SARAH's floating over my
bed as I sleep. Blood dripping from each of their palms - drip
dripping onto my face as I can do not but lie and watch as
they whisper - as they praise their DEMONIC PRINCE. As
they SHRIEK!

*She drops to her knees, grabs her head and
SCREAMS. Then, in a trance:*

ANN PUTNAM JR
Sarah Good. Sarah Osbourne. Both bow to Satan. But they
are not alone. I see so many shadowed figures kneeling
beside them. Some - who aren't even Sarah's...

REVEREND PARRIS
...How many?

ANN PUTNAM JR
Too many to count.

REVEREND PARRIS
Really?

THOMAS PUTNAM enters.

THOMAS PUTNAM
I'm afeared it be the case, *Sam*. Ann, sit with your friends.

ANN squeezes in with them.

ANN PUTNAM JR
Hello fellow children friends. How are you tod-
(She SCREAMS)
NOOOO! THEY CLAW AT ME! AT US! THE DARK
SPIRITS FIGHT TO KEEP US GIRLS APART! THEY
FEAR OUR POWER TOGETHER.

ABIGAIL WILLIAMS
...Oh no.

BETTY
Ohhhh geez.

MARY WARREN
Mary Warren, what have you got yourself into?

REVEREND PARRIS
Shut up, Mary! Abigail - What did you want to tell me?!

ABIGAIL WILLIAMS
We. Uhm. We. ...Ah....Uh. ...Hmmm.

ANN PUTNAM JR.
She's stricken mute! THE DEVIL draws her tongue down
her throat!

THOMAS PUTNAM
Magistrate. I've actually already put together a list of those
who sure sound like the vague figures ANN JR saw in her
dream.

PUTNAM unfurls a short list.

THE MAGISTRATE
Oh my. Mmmmm. Such delicious justice.

THOMAS PUTNAM
Let us send for Constable Wildes so he might arrest some witches and we can start some Witch Trials -

THE MAGISTRATE
CHILDREN with me. PARRIS, you too. I need someone to take the notes.

REVEREND PARRIS
Ooo, the most important job. Of course. Come, girls.

THE MAGISTRATE
AND BE PREPARED TO GIVE ME MORE NAMES!

THOMAS PUTNAM
Worry not The Magistrate - we all have many names to give. ...Ha. Hahaha. HAHAHA!

ALL follow off - MARY & ABIGAIL stop before they exit.

MARY WARREN
Is this a part of your plan?

ABIGAIL WILLIAMS
Obviously, NO, Mary.

MARY WARREN
They aim to *kill* people for this.

ABIGAIL WILLIAMS
Yeah. I heard!

MARY WARREN
So what do we do? How can we fix this?

ABIGAIL WILLIAMS
Fix this? Mary I - look. Maybe some of the adults deserve
punishment for once. How about that? What - we confess?
So WE become the ones to blame? I say we let the adults
handle it, like they always want to do. They're supposed to
know what's best for us. Right?

MARY WARREN
But -

ABIGAIL WILLIAMS
Why are you looking at me for any answers? *I'm twelve.*
                    (she begins to exit, turns:)
Twelve.

ABIGAIL follows. To us:

MARY WARREN
If there's a moral at the end of my story here - it's that a
social life is not worth the risk. Or it's to stay away from
eggs. Yeah. That's the takeaway.

MARY looks to a FROZEN BETTY.

BETTY PARRIS
So much pressure.

MARY WARREN
I only pray that if there truly be Witches amongst us - they
are discovered… Whomever they may be.

SCENE: WITCHES. IN SALEM.

Thunder. In darkness...

BELLA'LOCH & XANATAR
EVOCAMUS! CITAMUS SAPIDUM! CITAMUS
PODUM! EVOCAMUS!

A CAULDRON smokes. Lights on XANATAR &
BELLA.

BELLA'LOCH
Eye of a LIZARD! Spit of a WIZARD! From a book, a page.
One of those hats with a buckle that are all the hip rage!
Wing of Raven! Shell of snail! One hair from a Man named
John - so easy to find -

XANATAR
So easy.

XANATAR & BELLA'LOCH
DOUBLE DOUBLE! TOIL AND TROUBLE! FIRE BURN
AND -

A banging at the door.

BELLA'LOCH
Oh my - you don't suppose they've come for us?

XANATAR
Who? Shakespeare's copyright people? Fair use, I say!

EPHRAIM WILDES bursts on. He does not look
towards XANATAR and BELLA.

EPHRAIM
BY ORDER of THE MAGISTRATE you're under arrest for
WITCHCRAFT-

> *XANATAR and BELLA suddenly grab various*
> *magic items or weapons. BELLA mounts a*
> *broom.*

XANATAR & BELLA'LOCH
[Gasp.] OH NO! Whaaaat? No! NOOO! Wow! WOW WOW
WHAAA I'M SPEECHLESS?

EPHRAIM WILDES
How dare you corrupt the innocents of our village, Elizabeth
-
(he turns)
Wait - You're not Elizabeth Howe.

BELLA'LOCH
Oh!? No. Lizzy's house is the next over. The big lovely farm.
Not here. Not in our swamp hut. We're The Bloodkravens.

XANATAR
We're visiting Salem on an extended sojourn. We got a very
good discount from our travel agent.

EPHRAIM
Oh my gosh. I am so sorry. Look, it's been a rough few
weeks. The jails are getting full and everyone is mad at me
when I arrest their loved ones. Or when I arrest them
themselves.
(a beat)
I put handcuffs on my own mother this morning. She was
accused by Deliverance Hobbs who I arrested yesterday and
said "you'll regret this, CONSTABLE!" What did she mean
by that? How will I regret it?

XANATAR

Wow. Welp, good Morrow, our favorite of CONSTABLES!

EPHRAIM WILDES

Nice visiting ya, Bloodkravens! I wish everyone was more like you. Enjoy whatever you got brewin' there! So bubbly.

EPHRAIM leaves. They move back to the cauldron.

XANATAR

...Welp, dinner time.

They fill cups and drink.

XANATAR & BELLA'LOCH

Blegh. So much dog. Too much dog. Blegh.

SCENE: TRANSITION

EPHRAIM enters.

EPHRAIM WILDES

Elizabeth Howe?! Where are you? Please let me arrest you!

EDWARD BISHOP
(rushing on)
CONSTABLE WILDES! I found another WITCH! My neighbor, who's been CHOPPING DOWN TREES ON MY PROPERTY - His wife's a witch.

SARAH DUSTIN, a villager, rushes on.

SARAH DUSTIN

CONSTABLE! Thank you for what you're doing keeping us
safe. I, Sarah Dustin, would like to say a prayer for you.
OUR FATHER WHO ART IN HEAVEN. HALLOWED BE
YOUR NAME!

LYDIA DUSTIN, a different villager, enters.

LYDIA DUSTIN

Waaaiiit no - She said YOUR NAME. IT's THY NAME. It's
supposed to be THY. She's a witch! I, LYDIA DUSTIN,
knew it. I've never liked her. Must be because she's a witch!

SARAH DUSTIN

What? But we speak often. We're cousins! We're the
DUSTIN's! Please, let me say it again, I'll say thy.

*An UNNAMED VILLAGER jumps out - he
points to EDWARD.*

UNNAMED VILLAGER

CONSTABLE. This man, who keeps going on about TREES
I, a villager who will only appear in this scene therefore I do
not get name, HAVE A PERFECTLY LEGAL RIGHT TO
CHOP ON PROPERTY HIS FATHER SOLD TO MY
FATHER 25 YEARS AGO - his wife is a witch. And so is
that BRIDGET BISHOP woman - she's been making me
think some weird thoughts when I'm in bed at night and I'm
pretty sure that's not my fault.

PUTNAM enters.

THOMAS PUTNAM

I too have a few more names for you, Constable!

He unfurls the LONGEST list. ALL, and any

others available, swarm EPHRAIM.

ALL VILLAGERS OF SALEM
CONSTABLE! I've got a WITCH! WITCHES! MY
NEIGHBOR! MY WIFE! MY -

SCENE: SALEM WITCH EXAMINATIONS

MAGISTRATE bangs a gavel so much.
PUTNAM takes a SEAT in the front! PARRIS
takes notes.

THE MAGISTRATE
We, JOHN HATHORNE SLASH JOHN CORWIN welcome
YE to THESE SALEM WITCH TRIALS™. We shall BE
JOINED ON THIS COUNCIL OF NOT LAW BY THE
MINISTER SAMUEL SEWALL *HRGGH!* And JUDGE
THOMAS DANFORTH -
          (he procures a PERIWIG and puts it on)
....*Ahhhh.* BRING IN THE AFFLICTED!

ANN, ABIGAIL, a shaken BETTY, & MARY
enter.

THE MAGISTRATE
Ye have accused many of serving the DEVIL. But have ye
evidence of these witches' crimes?

ANN stands prominently. Each confession has
the air of a campfire ghost story. Perhaps with a
flashlight on their faces.

ANN PUTNAM JR.
I witnessed each and all's spirits consorting with the Devil.
At a Picnic - celebrating their Dark Lord. Rebecca Nurse

ANN PUTNAM JR. (CONT)
was there. And Sarah Good. And Sarah Osbourne. And more.
When they became aware I bore witness. THIS BITE did
they give me!

*She holds up her arm where a BITE MARK
exists. She very clearly gave herself this bite
moments ago. Gasps.*

ABIGAIL WILLIAMS
Yes AND *I* was pricked with this NEEDLE by an UNSEEN
force but they left the needle behind. Which makes sense!

She holds up a needle.

THE MAGISTRATE
Wow. Such evidence. MARY WARREN - What fantastical
and amazing thing has happened upon you?

LIGHTS shift on MARY. She speaks to us:

MARY WARREN
Hey. Mary Warren again. If you don't remember me, I'm
'Egg' girl. Believe you me, I tried to ignore all of this and go
back to life as usual at the PROCTORS. But Mr. Proctor, he
was all like "Stop this, Mary!" and I was like how - but
Elizabeth Proctor, that angel, she said 'there's another
judgment, dear child.' And she means THE FINAL
JUDGMENT. I have come to an accord with myself. I
started this. And today. I, Mary Warren, am going to end it.
Today. MARY WARREN brings the hammer dow-

Sudden shift back to the scene.

THE MAGISTRATE
I ASKED YE A QUESTION, WARREN!

MARY WARREN

Yes I was attacked by a sheet which was a witch. Here's a piece of the sheet which is proof.

THE MAGISTRATE

Wow. When you see it before your own eyes. Thank ye childr -

MARY WARREN

No. Stop. Stop all of this at once. I have a confess to do!

ABIGAIL WILLIAMS

Mary, can we talk out -

MARY WARREN

Shut up, Abigail! For I shall now deliver unto you all THE TRUTH. We afflicted do not but dis-

THOMAS PUTNAM

Uhhh - WAIT! STOP! What's that - something it's - attacking my daughter right now!

ANN PUTNAM JR

NO NO NO! GET AWAY!

THE MAGISTRATE

What. What is it?! WHAT DOTH YOU SEE? WHAT'S IN THE AIR?!

THOMAS PUTNAM

It's - It's -

BETTY PARRIS

IT'S - A BIG YELLOW BIRD!

Silence. All look to BETTY.

THOMAS PUTNAM
...a big yellow bird? Really?

BETTY PARRIS
Uh uhhh uhhh. Yeah. *So much pressure.*

THOMAS PUTNAM
Why - The most evil of sights to see! Big yellow birds. Woe.

REVEREND PARRIS
Where is this yellow bird now? For the court transcript? I'm
writing it, and I am loving my take on this.

ANN PUTNAM JR
THE YELLOW BIRD! Oh - It desires to fly to its evil
master.

Her finger falls on MARY WARREN.

THE MAGISTRATE
Let the invisible YELLOW BIRD be added to the court's
EVIDENCE! Mary Warren - explain yourself.

MARY WARREN
Abigail - please. Tell them the truth.

ABIGAIL WILLIAMS
...THE DEVIL made her do it. She put a curse on BETTY. I
SAW IT. The BIRD, flies to her.

ANN PUTNAM JR
HER BIRD PECKS AT MY EYES TO BLIND ME!

BETTY PARRIS
THE BIRD HAS A KNIFE! No! Don't pull out that that that
second knife?!

ABIGAIL WILLIAMS
THE DEVIL MADE HER DO IT. THE DEVIL. THE
DEVIL!!

ANN screams. ABIGAIL runs around.

THOMAS PUTNAM
WON'T SOMEONE save the Children from this dual
wielding BIRD?

THE MAGISTRATE
Children! Run! Run while you still can - Run before Witchy
Warren's YELLOW BIRD catches you.

> *Chaos as the girls run around and eventually
> exit.*

MARY WARREN
Please. It is sport to them. It is sport to us!

THE MAGISTRATE
Ephraim! Take the confessed shammer Mary Warren to
prison so she might learn to speak the TRUTH.

WILDES begins to drag her off.

EPHRAIM WILDES
/Maybe a bad time, but I haven't gotten paid by the
prisoners. They don't have money. K, Talk later!

MARY WARREN
/We dissembled! IT WAS SPORT! SPPOOORRT!

THE MAGISTRATE
Let's give her a week in prison? See if her story changes.

A beat. ALL wait. Gavels!

THE MAGISTRATE
Oops, it's been THREE weeks. BRING WARREN BACK IN!

*MARY enters. Dirty. Chained. Her emotions
have fled her human vessel. A terrifying quick
change.*

THE MAGISTRATE
What say ye now, Warren?

MARY WARREN
...I signed the Devil's book. Mister Proctor brought it to me.
He's a witch like his nice wife. Oh look. I have here another
list of confirmed witches I saw in my dreams that weren't
dreams but were real life.

THE MAGISTRATE
Warren, thank ye. Ye may rejoin your friends in accusing
witches. After, one more week in prison.

He goes to GAVEL - A shift. MARY, to us:

MARY WARREN
Another lesson for you - I have found there is much
difficulty in saying what is agreed to be 'the right thing'. Yet
other words speak so much easier. No one cares when you
say those words. So, why not alway say those easy ones?

MARY WARREN (CONT)

They are easier after all. I hope you leave here having
learned a lesson.
(she begins laughing)
Pardon me. None of this is that word that means when
something makes you laugh. But it is ridiculous.

MARY exits. THE MAGISTRATE bangs a gavel.

THE MAGISTRATE

NOW - I: John Hathorne, George Corwin, Samuel Sewall,
and Thomas Danforth am now joined by the honorable
Magistrate William Stoughton -
(horrific shift)
The final piece - *Gaaah HELLFIRE! GUILTY!*
(a second PERIWIG falls on his head.)
PRESIDING. We shall now bring out the AFFLICTERS.
These TRIALS - SHALL be FAIR and JUST. And so a jury
of your unbiased peers have been assembled from within the
VILLAGE to render a verdict. Bring in THE IMPARTIAL
JURY!

XANATAR & BELLA enter.

BELLA'LOCH

Gooood Morrow neighbors! Happy to be jury-ing.
Impartially! What a surprise to be asked!

XANATAR

Can't wait to be IMPARTIAL about who is or is not a witch.

THE MAGISTRATE

BRIDGET BISHOP.
(Bridget enters)
YE have been accused of Witchcraft. What have YE to say?

BRIDGET BISHOP

We've been through this before. I'm not a witch. I don't even know what we're saying a witch is.

THE MAGISTRATE

So how do you know if you're not a witch?

BRIDGET BISHOP

I don't understand the question.

THE MAGISTRATE

It's simple. How do you not not know if you're not NOT a not witch? ...Jury?

XANATAR & BELLA'LOCH

GUILTY.

BRIDGET BISHOP

Please! Does no one remember -

> *BANG! CRASH! CREAK. A silhouette of a body hangs from a tree. The silhouette sways back and forth for a good long while.*
>
> *Lights. A gasp from BRIDGET. She looks around, isolated.*

BRIDGET BISHOP

I remember. Dying, that is. I remember it being terrible. I remember thinking, hoping, praying even in those last few seconds that even though it all felt so pointless, so wrong. That one day, there'd be some good reason for it. And suddenly - in the blink of an eye - I'm back in SALEM. It seems generations have passed. First I see, near the very spot I died - tucked away in a quaint little backstreet. There is a small monument. My name is on it. That's a start. Twenty

BRIDGET BISHOP (CONT)

four other names are too. This quaint memorial is eclipsed by a large building nearby - a building built right on the very spot I died. Emblazoned in bright heavenly light is its name: WALGREENS.

(a beat)

I enter this Walgreens, and suddenly I'm standing in the very spot where the wagon I was carted on from the jail stopped and they made me trudge through mud up a hill - I had not eaten for days. In this WALL of GREENs I realize I see many people. Many women. And they wear such colors. One is in red. She stands in the same place my old neighbor spit in my face and called me a Witch - next to many cylinders of something called Pringles. Moving further in - near the spot where I climbed a ladder, a noose was put around my neck, and I was pushed and I choked and choked for a long while because they hadn't quite tied the noose right, which I don't blame them for, they hadn't really ever practiced before. Okay, maybe I did blame them a little in the moment - but. *I got over it.* In that spot is something called a seasonal aisle. And huh. Lots of witch imagery, I notice. Odd. All kinds of witch clothings. Some with large warted noses. Others are labeled as 'sexy witch.' I flee this Walgreen for it is giving me frights - but oh no - in the streets. There are nothing BUT witches all around. I arrive at a STATUE in the town square! Aw, a woman - named Samatha Stevens. BUT O NO! It says she is BEWITCHED! Satan's imagery emblazons articles of clothing in every window - around each and every corner I spy MORE JOVIAL WITCHES. Many of them the labeled SEXY VARIETY. What is this? Why is this? Did - did the witches win? Everywhere I turn that which I was murdered for is celebrated on every street, and - ohhh. Of course.

(a beat)

Hell. This must be hell. That makes so much more sense. ...I can only pray the real world is better.

SCENE: THE TRYALS CONTINUED

GAVEL GAVEL GAVEL.

THOMAS PUTNAM
BEGIN NOW THE TRYAL OF GOODY GOOD!

GOODY GOOD
Yesss? NO! Curse you Putnam. Curse you all! You take my
life away - God will give you BLOOD TO DRINK! He'll get
you. He'll get you *GOOD. YEESSSS HE WILL.*

XANATAR & BELLA'LOCH
That sounds very GUILTY!

CLANG. A hanging shadow appears.

REVEREND PARRIS
Martha Corey.

MARTHA enters.

MARTHA COREY
I am an innocent person. I never had anything to do with
witchcraft since I was born. I am a gospel woman. I tell you
the very truth of it all - and you will murder me for it.

THE MAGISTRATE
Maybe. Maybe not. Jury?

XANATAR & BELLA'LOCH
....Guilty.

THE MAGISTRATE
Maybe it is!

CLANG. Another hanging shadow appears.

THE MAGISTRATE & PARRIS & PUTNAM
REBECCA NURSE...

> *Rebecca Nurse is lead on by EPHRAIM. So dirty.*

REBECCA NURSE
I am sorry to bring it up, but I think there was a mix up and I was accidentally imprisoned for months...

THE MAGISTRATE
I've heard enough. JURY - what say ye?

> *BELLA & XANATAR whisper back and forth until agreement.*

BELLA'LOCH
We, the jury, do find Rebecca Nurse...

XANATAR & BELLA'LOCH
......NOT guilty.

THE MAGISTRATE
I am not satisfied with this verdict. I'd like another.

> *The two confer again.*

XANATAR
We're still leaning towards Not GUILTY.

THE MAGISTRATE
I would like a different verdict, please.

They confer.

XANATAR

Innocent?

THE MAGISTRATE

Not quite what I'm after.

BELLA'LOCH

Rebecca Nurse be NOT a witch.

THE MAGISTRATE

I SAID I WOULD LIKE ANOTHER VERDICT.

BELLA'LOCH & XANATAR

Guilty?

THE MAGISTRATE

...guilty.

Gavel.

REBECCA NURSE

Excuse me. Everyone seems upset. Please - whatever it is
that's got you in turmoil - don't let it destroy you. That's not
who you are. That's a sickness inside you and it needs
treatment. It needs a little thing called loving thy neighbor.
Because if you can find it in you to love just one person.
Then they might love you. And if one person loves you.
Then that's proof enough that someone else can. So someone
else will. And on it will go - over and over until ...Paradise.
                    (a beat)
Now can someone tell me when I get to go home?

CLANG. A hanging shadow.

THE MAGISTRATE
SUSANNAH MARTIN! ELIZABETH HOWE! SARAH
WILDES - Don't bother bringing them in. Jury?

XANATAR & BELLA'LOCH
....Guilty guilty guilty?

CLANG CLANG CLANG. MORE shadows.

SCENE: JOHN PROCTOR AT THE GALLOWS

PROCTOR enters. He speaks to us.

JOHN PROCTOR
Before I go, I know everyone out there is thinking - what has
JOHN PROCTOR been doing this whole time. The truth is:
Not much. But if you'll allow me this one FINAL
MONOLOGUE. First - I'm innocent, but more importantly,
I, JOHN PROCTOR, DID NOT HAVE A RELATIONSHIP
WITH A TWELVE YEAR OLD GIRL. Please, if anyone
revisits all of this hundreds of years from now for some
horrible reason, don't make that a whole thing. Maybe if you
age her up in that version - No, I said it out loud and I don't
like it. It's my name. I don't get another. End mono-

Clang. A shadow hangs.

SCENE: THE GIRLS AGAIN

*ABIGAIL, BETTY and MARY stand looking to
the shadow as it fades. Eventually, ABIGAIL
procures a glass and an egg.*

ABIGAIL WILLIAMS
Hey. You two want to put an egg in a glass? See what our future's hold?

ABIGAIL cracks an 'egg' into the glass.

BETTY PARRIS
I see ...I think... I think it's a shoe? My future husband is a shoemaker? ...I hate it.

MARY WARREN
I don't see anything. It's just an egg.

ABIGAIL WILLIAMS
............I see a coffin.

ANN PUTNAM JR. enters, carrying a bird.

ANN PUTNAM JR
Best friends. Look what I found - A new bird! For my collection...

She kneels and does her thing with the birds. The others back away.

ABIGAIL WILLIAMS
Wow. She's a lot, huh?

MARY WARREN
Her? We all are.

BETTY PARRIS
Abigail, is this still part of the plan? Is the plan that we do this forever?

ABIGAIL WILLIAMS

When was the last time you sewed? Folded something? Were told to shut up? …Not like we can end it anyways. Not like there's one powerful rich person who could snap their fingers and - wait. That could work. No. Maybe. First thought best thought.

ABIGAIL looks to BETTY & MARY. She nods. SCREAMS. ANN JR. Looks to her.

ANN PUTNAM JR

What?

ABIGAIL WILLIAMS

You see it - don't you?! RIGHT THERE. ANN, you have to see it. She points a bloody finger at you.

ANN PUTNAM JR

…who is it?

ABIGAIL whispers in her ear. ANN JR is very worried. All whisper.

ABIGAIL & ANN JR & BETTY & MARY

WE SAW MARY PHIPS, wife of MASSACHUSETTS GOVERNOR WILLIAM PHIPS, with THE DEVIL!

SCENE: THE END OF THE SALEM WITCH TRIALS

TRUMPETS! GOVERNOR PHIPS, a real dandy gentleman, powerful, a politician, enters.

GOVERNOR PHIPS

Woah woah woah! Hello everyone in Massahookets - It's

GOVERNOR PHIPS (CONT)
me! Governor Phips. A'thank you! I say - Apparently, MY
OWN WIFE, yes, as in:
(Borat)
MAH WIIIIFE, has been accused in this whole Sallem Witch
thing. A line has been crossed. So. That's done now. I'm
calling the whole thing off.

*PARRIS, THE MAGISTRATE & THOMAS
PUTNAM rush on.*

ALL
What?! NO - That can't be! [etc.]

THOMAS PUTNAM
Governor! Please. You must stay the course.

GOVERNOR PHIPS
Who's this guy?

THOMAS PUTNAM
Who? Who am - Who am I? Ha! HAHA! Who am I? *WHO
AM I?!* MY DAUGHTER has been ATTACKED. BY spirits!
And ghosts! And birds - it's hard to keep up! ANN JR.
Quick!

REVEREND PARRIS
ABIGAIL! You too!

ANN JR. & ABIGAIL enter.

THOMAS PUTNAM
Tell Governor Phips YOU didn't mean to accuse HIS wife, it
was a uh, different Governor - or -

ABIGAIL

No! And leave herself open to the EVILs Mary Phips aims to cast upon her?!

ANN PUTNAM JR

No. NO I cannot. I WILL NOT!

ABIGAIL

You have to hang on until the end of days, ANN!

ANN PUTNAM JR

"The cowardly, the unbelieving, the vile, the murderers, the sexually immoral, SORCERERS, and all LIARS - their place will be in the lake of FIRE." Revelation 21:8.

REVEREND PARRIS

Woaaaah! Spoilers! Some of us aren't there yet!

THOMAS PUTNAM

ANN. Stop it. Stop this at once.

ABIGAIL

Beware, Ann. No one is safe from the DEVIL and his ilk! O! I fear Satan's servants may be in this room right now! They SURROUND US. Could it even be - UNCLE PARRIS?! OR MISTER PUTNAM?!

THOMAS PUTNAM

No! It's not! PARRIS - CONTROL your child!

They girls continue to shriek and point. They take up more and more space - the others, frightened at the scene, huddle close together. PHIPS steps out.

GOVERNOR PHIPS

OKAAAAY. Wow. Up close it is - dramatic. Thank you, you childs, for all your work. You can grab a lollipop on your way out.

ANN PUTNAM JR

[Shrieks.]

GOVERNOR PHIPS

YOU JUST LOST YOUR LOLLIPOP. Get her out of here.

THOMAS PUTNAM

Ann Jr. You've ruined everything. Go lock yourself in your room again. NOW.

ANN PUTNAM JR

I'm. I'm sorry Mr. Thomas Putnam.

ANN JR hangs her head and exits.

ABIGAIL

So sorry, ...Uncle.

ABIGAIL smirks and exits.

THE MAGISTRATE

What of the many found guilty already of Witchcraft? They are set to hang in the coming weeks. We can't go back on that. That's THE LAW.

GOVERNOR PHIPS

Fine. We finish them out - Bing bang boom. Yeah?

One BIG CLANG. Many hanging silhouettes. So many.

GOVERNOR PHIPS
K. Now we're done. Oof. This job is stressful. I'm off to
Martha's Vineyard. Someone go tell my wife she's off the
hook. K. Bye.

He exits. PARRIS hugs his wood close.

THE MAGISTRATE
We need more trials. We need more Justice. We feel so
COLD. PARRIS? Give us that wood.

REVEREND PARRIS
THIS IS MY WOOD, IT WILL NEVER WARM YOU.

*MAGISTRATE moves to grab it - PARRIS
FIGHTS BACK. PUTNAM breaks up the
conflict.*

THOMAS PUTNAM
Parris. Magistrate. Remember your GODLINESS! Then give
the wood to me - it's Putnam wood! From Putnam Land!

*PUTNAM attempts to pry the wood from
PARRIS.*

REVEREND PARRIS
No!

A petty struggle begins between them all.

THE MAGISTRATE
GIVE IT! WE EARNED IT! WE TRIED SO MANY!

REVEREND PARRIS
I EARNED IT BY BEING EVERYONE'S FAVORITE
REVEREND!

THOMAS PUTNAM
I EARNED IT WHEN MY GRANDFATHER EARNED IT!

More sad struggle. More sad physical activity
one could barely call fighting . Nothing about it
is an epic showdown. Eventually they fall to the
ground so out of breath from this tiniest bit of
activity.

PUTNAM / PARRIS / MAGISTRATE
Give it! Ahh! ooo! STOP! OW! OW! OW! *[etc.]*

A long beat. Heavy breathing from the ground
from all. Eventually, PARRIS sits up.

REVEREND PARRIS
Perhaps. I shall admit. It all got out of hand. Barely.

THE MAGISTRATE
A tiny bit. But you need this kind of distance from it to
realize that. PERSPECTIVE.

THOMAS PUTNAM
Actually - There's a lesson to be learned here. A valuable
one.. ...*This* is why we can't trust Women.

REVEREND PARRIS
Yes. So true. That is the lesson.

THOMAS PUTNAM
And those children really manipulated us, huh?

REVEREND PARRIS

ABIGAIL, her and John Proctor seemed to have some sort of
- thing? I think that's a reason for this.

THE MAGISTRATE

We're pretty sure we had some bad rye bread the other day.
MAYBE all this was caused by bad bread?

REVEREND PARRIS

Yes. That is a good theory.

THOMAS PUTNAM

Bread Poisoning. Children. Love between a sixty year old
man and a twelve year old girl. And women.

THE MAGISTRATE

Yep. That's what this was. So ordered. ... You know, this was
a fine time. We should do it again. SOON.

ALL THREE

Well. Good morrow, then!

All nod. All exit. A long beat.

THOMAS PUTNAM (O.S.)
Wait. Agh! AGH NO NO WAIT WAIT WAIT!!
(he re-enters)

THOMAS PUTNAM

PORTER! I ACCUSE The Porters of being witches! We
can't forget them! GIRLS! COME BACK! GOVERNOR!
MAGISTRATE, GIVE ME THEIR LANDS! PARRIS -
BACK ME UP! GIRLS! TELL EVERYONE! HANG THE
PORTERS! PLEASE! YOU KNOW WHAT THEY DID.
WE ALL KNOW WHAT THE PORTERS DID...

PARRIS has re-entered during this.

REVEREND PARRIS
Thomas. It's over. It's all over now. This is… how it ends.

PARRIS sighs and exits.

THOMAS PUTNAM
PORRRRRTTTTEEEEERRR.

SCENE: BOWS

> *The COMPANY stands. No frills. No smiling faces. Just sadness. No bows even. Just IMPORTANCE. Eventually, lights shift to BELLA & XANATAR*

BELLA'LOCH
Wow. Wow wow. This all sure turned out to be a real downer, didn't it Xanatar?

XANATAR
Yeah. It really did.

BELLA'LOCH
So sad. …Xanatar - you don't think - Nah.

XANATAR
What?

BELLA'LOCH
You don't think maaaybe - we could have, I don't know. Done something?

XANATAR

Ha! You mean like we could have used our tremendous
powers plucked from the weave of all living things to HELP
the oppressed people of this vill- You know, now that I've
said it out loud - yeah we could have done that.

BELLA'LOCH

...Maybe We still could. You thinking what I'm thinking?

XANATAR & BELLA'LOCH

TIME SPELL!
            (lights flash)
Ooo! We're traveling in time - back in time -

XANATAR

TIME MAGIC - Oooo! Using magic we can travel back in
time! It's something we can do! We could always do it!

XANATAR & BELLA

TRAVELING BACK TO THE TRIAL OF -

SCENE: TRIAL OF BRIDGET BISHOP (REVISITED)

We're back at the MEETINGHOUSE.

*[A note on this final scene. First off, congrats on
making it this far. Hope you've had a fun but
also upsetting time. What you are about to read
is written out to be technically ambitious. We
often would joke that a production essentially
wants to save the majority of the budget for this
ending spectacle.*

*However! What is stated in the stage directions
here is simply a suggestion, as it is with all
things. All that matters is that those who we
have been watching as 'the perpetrators' get the
comeuppance they never received in history. It is
intended to be over the top and violent in almost
a cartoonish way, maybe even crossing the line
of 'how fun' into 'too much.' The hangings were
something the villagers gathered to watch, to
consume - a chance to see people they were told
were evil be punished. This scene is going for
that same set of feelings - the good ones and the
bad ones one may feel when witnessing violence.
Have fun, go wild.]*

THE MAGISTRATE
BRIDGET BISHOP!

BRIDGET BISHOP
Yeah?

THE MAGISTRATE
I PRONOUNCE YE GUIILLLLL-

BELLA'LOCH
HOLD! We demand this TRYAL concluded!

XANATAR
FOR WE ALL KNOW this be WRONG! We shan't stand
aside and allow it. And we never would - no one can prove
otherwise.

REVEREND PARRIS
Goody BloodKraven! Mister BloodKraven! What is this
about?

XANTAR
We have a CONFESSION for YE!

BELLA'LOCH
That WE, THE BLOODKRAVENS BE -

XANATAR & BELLA'LOCH
WITCHES! IN SALEM HE HE HE!

ALL ON STAGE
WITCHES?! IN SALEM!?

THE MAGISTRATE
THEY SHAM US NOT! EPHRAIM! ARREST THESE
WITCHES!

*EPHRAIM moves to arrest them. BELLA waves
a STAFF at him. LIGHTS flash!*

EPHRAIM WILDES
OH! MY! GOOOOO-

*A skeleton stands where he once stood. ALL
scream.*

THE MAGISTRATE
STOP THESE MAGICKS! STOP AT ONCE! I ORDER Y-

*XANATAR waves his hands at the
MAGISTRATE. He gurgles. He chokes. He dies.*

GOODY GOOD
HAHAHA! He choked on Blood! Got him! GOT HIM
GOOD! YEEEEESSSSS!!!!!!

SPIRITS fly around the theater. CROWS.
RAVENS. DEMONS. PARRIS stumbles to the
center, holding up firewood.

REVEREND PARRIS
STOP! PLEASE! I REBUKE YE!

XANATAR
DAEMON DAEMONIUM! BY BLOOD WE SUMMON
THEE FROM THE PITS BEYOND!

BELLA & XANATAR do a spell - THE WALLS
OF THE THEATER CRACK OPEN AS A
HIDEOUS BEAST FROM BEYOND GRABS
PARRIS and DRAGS HIM OFF STAGE.

REVEREND PARRIS
Nooooooo!

THE THREE turn towards PUTNAM, now with
knives.

THOMAS PUTNAM
I was just a concerned parent! I did nothing wrong. This is
ATROCIOUS. This is a WITCH LOOKY LOOK Look
wronging a RIGHTEO-

BELLA AND XANATAR wave hands as
ABIGAIL, ANN, BETTY and MARY get to
Caesaring him.

ANN PUTNAM JR
HAHAHAHAHAHAHAHAHAHAHAHAHAHAHAHAH
AHAHAHAHA! I'M FREE! FREEE!

BELLA'LOCH

INNOCENT VILLAGERS! Emotionally abused accusers!
SLIGHTLY CULPABLE BYSTANDERS! Let us away! TO
SAFETY! TO THE WOOOODS!

> *Whoosh. We're in 'THE WOODS.' ALL but
> Xanatar & Bella look around, very confused. A
> little frightened.*

XANATAR

The nice safe woods. No one can hurt you now. Except us.
HAHA! But we won't. Unless! I'm kidding.

BELLA'LOCH

Who's up for a lil' woods Dance? Huh?! *That's a thing we
witches do! Come on!*

> *MUSIC. They start dancing. All look on in
> horror.*

XANATAR

No one's dancing! COME ON! Celebrate! You're free!
You're not afraid of some WITCHES are you?! DANCE!
EVERYBODY DANCE!

> *Music. BELLA and XANATAR dance. The others
> look around confused. Xanatar and BELLA
> dance while villagers look at them in horror.
> Eventually, with a pose.*

BELLA'LOCH & XANATAR

Hahaha - WITCHES! IN SALEM!

> *Blackout. End of play.*

www.ingramcontent.com/pod-product-compliance
Lightning Source LLC
Chambersburg PA
CBHW031231120626
46545CB00003B/1076